Ulysses S. Grant
General and President

Susan Bachner

Boston, Massachusetts
Chandler, Arizona
Glenview, Illinois
Upper Saddle River, New Jersey

Illustrations

2, 5, 8 John White; 7 Joe LeMonnier.

Photographs

Every effort has been made to secure permission and provide appropriate credit for photographic material. The publisher deeply regrets any omission and pledges to correct errors called to its attention in subsequent editions.

Unless otherwise acknowledged, all photographs are the property of Pearson Education, Inc.

Photo locators denoted as follows: Top (T), Center (C), Bottom (B), Left (L), Right (R), Background (Bkgd)

Opener: Prints & Photographs Division, LC-DIG-pga-02027/Library of Congress; 1 Prints & Photographs Division, LC-DIG-pga-02027/Library of Congress; 3 Prints & Photographs Division, LC-USZ62-101867/Library of Congress; 4 Prints & Photographs Division, LC-DIG-pga-02027/Library of Congress; 6 Prints & Photographs Division, LC-DIG-pga-01849/Library of Congress; 9 Prints & Photographs Division, LC-USZ62-90668/Library of Congress; 10 Prints & Photographs Division, LC-DIG-pga-03461/Library of Congress; 11 Prints & Photographs Division, LC-USZC4-2399/Library of Congress; 12 Prints & Photographs Division, LC-USZ62-37423/Library of Congress; 13 Prints & Photographs Division, LC-USZC4-5606/Library of Congress; 14 Prints & Photographs Division, LC-USZ62-7607/Library of Congress; 15 Prints & Photographs Division, LC-USZ6-2072/Library of Congress.

ISBN-13: 978-0-328-67705-4
ISBN-10:   0-328-67705-1

11 12 13 V0SI 18 17 16 15

The Rise of Ulysses S. Grant

When the Civil War began in 1861, Ulysses Grant was working in his father's store. He was 39 and had failed at several careers. For Grant, the future did not look bright.

However, the Civil War provided Grant with a career and a chance to help his country. By 1865, he was a military hero. And in 1868 he was elected president of the United States. How did this unlikely hero get his start?

Childhood

Ulysses S. Grant was born Hiram Ulysses Grant on April 27, 1822, in Point Pleasant, Ohio. Grant's father, Jesse, owned a leather shop. Everyone in the family helped run the shop—all but Ulysses. He preferred working with his father's horses.

At school, Grant was an average student. His father thought he needed discipline, so he enrolled Grant in the Military Academy of West Point, New York. Grant did not look forward to military school. However, he knew it was the only way he could continue his education. At the academy, school records incorrectly changed his name to U. S. Grant. The name stuck.

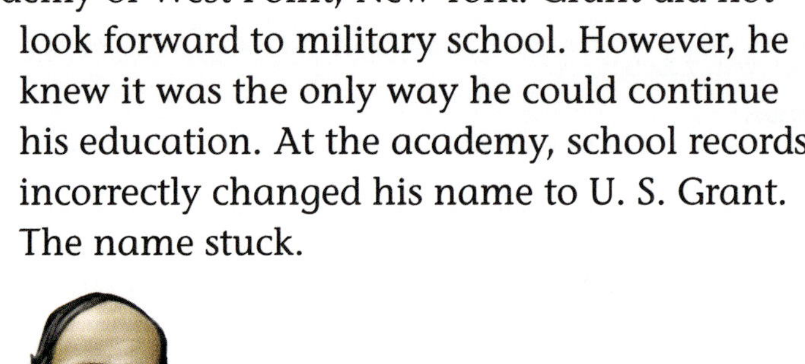

Grant's parents were Jesse Root Grant and Hannah Simpson Grant.

2

The West Point Years

Grant did not like the Military Academy and did not do well there. He dressed sloppily and slouched when he was supposed to stand up straight. Later, he wrote, "A military life had no charms for me, and I had not the faintest idea of staying in the army." Grant read a lot and excelled in math. In 1843, he graduated in twenty-first place out of a class of 39.

After graduation, Grant joined the army and was sent to Missouri. There, he met Julia Dent, the sister of his West Point roommate. While Grant was shy and awkward, Julia was outgoing and friendly. The two soon fell in love.

Ulysses Grant asked Julia Dent to marry him, but marriage would have to wait. First, the young army officer was called to serve his country in the Mexican War.

The Mexican War

Between 1846 and 1848, the United States was at war with Mexico. The conflict was mostly about land. By the end of the war, the United States had gained a large area of Mexico's land, including what is now the southwestern United States.

As a young soldier, Grant performed several jobs during the Mexican War, including keeping track of supplies for the troops. Grant did well at this job because it required him to be organized and use his math skills. But he preferred to fight and yearned to be sent to battle.

When Grant finally did fight, he showed great courage on the battlefield and was **promoted**. But he had mixed feelings about the war. Later, he wrote, "I do not think there ever was a more wicked war than that waged by the United States in Mexico."

Grant was a young man when he fought in the Mexican War.

Married Life

In 1848, when the Mexican War was over, Grant married Julia Dent. At first, the new bride followed her husband to wherever he was sent. But sometimes, Grant had to leave his wife alone for weeks. The time apart was difficult for them.

In 1853, Grant was assigned to Fort Humboldt, California. Grant and his wife had two young sons by this time. Grant had to go to California without his family. The loneliness was too much for him. In 1854, he resigned from the army.

Over the next few years, Grant worked at several jobs. He invested money in a business, but he lost all his money. He tried farming, but the farm failed. He even worked selling land and houses in St. Louis. But he was just not a good salesman.

Finally, having nowhere else to go, Grant moved to Galena, Illinois, where his parents lived. As a young man, he had avoided working in his father's leather shop. But now Grant had no choice—he had a family to support. In 1860, at the age of 38, Grant took a job with his father.

The Civil War

When the Civil War began, in April 1861, Grant returned to the army. He organized and trained volunteer troops for the Union army in Galena, Illinois. As commander of an Illinois regiment, or group, of about 1,000 soldiers, his first task was to face the Confederates in Missouri. In July, he nervously marched toward a Confederate camp. Finding the camp empty, Grant realized that the enemy had fled out of fear. He later wrote that the Confederate commander "had been as much afraid of me as I had been of him."

Victory in Tennessee

Grant's actions in Missouri earned him a promotion— and a new mission. His task was to recapture Fort Henry and Fort Donelson in Tennessee. In February 1862, after forcing the enemy to give up Fort Henry, Grant surrounded Fort Donelson. The Confederate soldiers fought hard, but Grant's troops won.

When Grant met the Confederate commander at Fort Donelson, Grant insisted on "unconditional surrender." This meant that he would make no deals with the commander. Word soon spread about Grant's victory. He became a hero. People began calling him "Unconditional Surrender" Grant.

The Battle of Fort Donelson was the first major victory for both Grant and the Union.

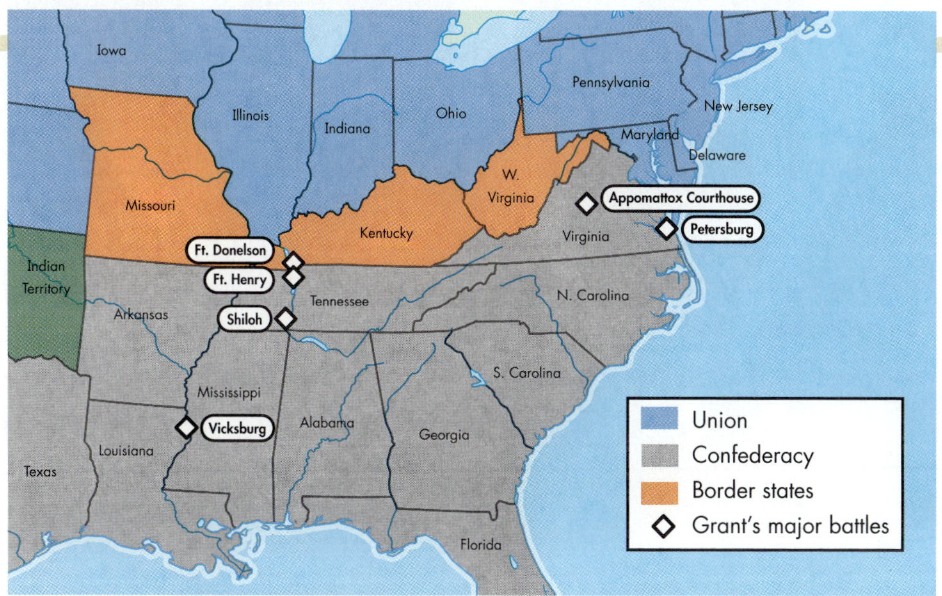

The Battle of Shiloh

After his success, Grant sought to clear the Confederate army out of Tennessee. But on April 6, 1862, Confederate troops launched a surprise attack on Grant's troops. During the Battle of Shiloh, as it came to be called, Grant's men were pushed against the Tennessee River. Defeat was near. But Grant fought on, forcing the Confederates back. The Union finally won the battle but at a huge cost. More than 10,000 Union soldiers and as many Confederate soldiers died. People were shocked at the number of dead. Some Northerners were so angry that they called for Grant to be fired. But Lincoln defended his general. "I can't spare this man," Lincoln told his critics. "He fights."

Grant at Vicksburg

The next opportunity for Grant came at Vicksburg, Mississippi. Vicksburg was important because it was where the Confederate army supplies were kept. On July 4, 1863, Grant captured Vicksburg and cut off Confederate supplies. It was a crushing blow to the South.

The End of the Civil War

In late 1863, President Lincoln promoted Grant to the role of top commander of the Union forces. Grant's mission was to bring the war to an end with a victory for the North. His plan was to put pressure on Confederate troops everywhere at once. "Give the enemy no rest," he ordered. The plan took time and resulted in many deaths, but it worked. On April 9, 1865, the highest Confederate commander, General Robert E. Lee, surrendered to Grant at Appomattox Court House in Virginia.

The war was over, but the country had been torn apart, and thousands had lost their lives. Grant knew that the two sides would have to forgive each other for the nation to move forward. He asked Confederate soldiers to give up their weapons and vow never again to fight against the government. Then, he allowed them to go home.

After the War

A few days after Lee's surrender, President Lincoln was shot and killed. Andrew Johnson became president. Though many Northerners wanted to punish the South after the war, Johnson, like Grant, urged forgiveness. The president did not agree with Grant on one important point. Grant believed that African American men should be given voting rights. Johnson did not.

By 1868, Grant was still a popular general, touring the South as part of **Reconstruction**. But the Congress, and much of the public, had lost faith in Johnson. They wanted a new leader. And they found one in Ulysses Grant. Grant ran for president that year. His slogan, "Let us have peace," showed his desire to heal the country from the wounds of the war.

Grant's campaign poster for the 1868 election

Grant and Lincoln

President Lincoln respected and admired General Grant. It was not surprising that the President would ask Grant and his wife to accompany him and Mrs. Lincoln to Ford's Theatre to watch a play. The Grants could not accept the invitation. Tragically, President Lincoln and his wife did attend the theatre the night of April 14, 1865. During the play, John Wilkes Booth, a supporter of the Confederacy, walked into the president's box and shot him. Lincoln died the next morning.

The Presidency

Grant won the election and was **inaugurated** president of the United States in 1869. He was 46 years old, the youngest man yet to be elected president.

When Grant and his family moved into the White House, they lived in fine style. Newspapers published details of fancy state dinners and the wedding of his daughter, Nellie, who was married in the White House. The public seemed to love the Grant family.

President Grant was popular, too. However, he was not experienced in politics, and it showed. He gave political jobs to friends instead of more qualified people. These blunders became costly political mistakes later on.

Civil Rights

One of the goals of Reconstruction was to help African American people who had been freed from slavery. But this goal angered many Southern white people. Some even began to threaten and harm African Americans. As a result, Grant pushed for passage of the Fifteenth Amendment in 1870, which guaranteed voting rights for African American men. Then he urged the passage of two **civil rights** acts. The first sought to protect African American people from violence, while the second outlawed **segregation**. However, these laws were often not enforced.

Grant also tried to help Native Americans. He brought about changes that resulted in better education, health care, and housing for Native American people.

The Panic of 1873

Grant's first term in office went fairly well. The **economy** was gaining strength. The country seemed to be healing from the Civil War. Grant was popular and was easily reelected in 1872.

But then, disaster struck. In 1873, some businesses ran out of money and stopped paying their bills. Americans began to panic as people everywhere began to lose money. Prices of crops dropped, and some farmers lost their farms. Workers lost their jobs. This **recession** became known as the Panic of 1873.

Grant had to act to improve the situation. In 1874, he **vetoed** a bill that would have increased the amount of paper money available. Increasing the amount of paper money reduces the value of that money. Grant's move was a smart one since it helped protect the value of American money. It also gave Americans confidence in the economy, which soon began to improve.

Scandals

By all accounts, Ulysses S. Grant was an honest man. However, some of the people around him were not as honest. As a result, there were **scandals** during his presidency.

The first scandal erupted in 1872. Some congressmen from Grant's party had taken **bribes**. Newspapers published details of the scandal, which deeply embarrassed Grant.

Then, in 1875, government workers were caught keeping tax money from alcohol sales. These people were named "the Whiskey Ring." Grant, himself, was not accused and he tried hard to show that he was not connected with the scandal. He told the public, "Let no guilty man escape." No sooner had he made the statement than his own secretary was accused of being involved.

By the time Grant finished his second term in office, he was discouraged. He had been honest and worked hard to make the country better. But he realized his presidency would be remembered more for its scandals than its achievements.

This political cartoon shows Grant being pulled down by the weight of scandal.

After the Presidency

After leaving office in 1877, the Grants set out on a two-year trip around the world. In 1881, two years after their return, they moved to New York City. They wanted to live near their son, Ulysses Jr., who was a partner in a business there. Encouraged by their son, the Grants invested all their money in the business. But in 1884, the other partner stole the company's money, leaving the Grants with nothing.

To support his family, Grant began writing articles about his war experiences. To his surprise, the articles were popular. Grant began writing his **memoirs** about military life.

A year into his new writing career, Grant began having throat pain. Doctors told him he had throat cancer.

Knowing he had little time left, Grant worked hard on his memoirs. He wrote constantly in the last days of his life. He finished his memoirs before he died on July 23, 1885.

In spite of his illness, Grant wrote constantly to finish his memoirs before he died.